Misadventures in Mommyhood
the truth & nothing but the truth
(so PLEASE help me God)
a compilation of tales by Kristin Quinn

For my mother ...

(because now I know)

Copyright © 2013 by Barefoot Ventures, LLC

Cover by: Photography by KLC

All rights reserved. No part of this book may be reproduced in any form by any electronic or mechanical means including photocopying, recording, or information storage and retrieval without permission in writing from the author.

ISBN-13: 978-1-484-180587
ISBN-10: 1-484-180585

Book Website
misadventuresinmommyhood.com
Email: kqsales@gmail.com

Printed in U.S.A

A quick introduction...

Why wouldn't you go into pregnancy, delivery, and motherhood headstrong and cocky? You don't know any better. And then you get smacked in the face with a billy club. Follow along one woman's humbling, honest, horrifying, yet hilarious misadventures in mommyhood. The truth & nothing but the truth on all things MOMMYHOOD. Get real.

Follow my blog:
www.misadventuresinmommyhood.com

Follow me on Facebook:
www.facebook.com
/MisadventuresInMommyhood

chapter one

baby ♡

TALES FROM THE HOSPITAL BED

chapter one
baby ♡

Your hospital bed checklist, pre-birth.

1.) Expect nothing and then everything will go as planned.

2.) Have chapstick at the ready.

3.) Be kind to your husband, no matter what.

4.) Let him watch sports in the delivery room. It helps take his mind of seeing you in pain and you might have a great story afterwards: Little Miss was born during a Bruins game, we will never forget that game. They went on to win the Stanley Cup.

5.) Be nice to the nurses even if they aren't nice to you. They do most of the work. They have seen and heard everything. You want them on your side... literally and figuratively.

6.) Put a cute headband on. If you forgot one have your mom bring you one. When you get your post delivery picture taken everyone will comment on how adorable you look. (Its the little things).

7.) Get a pedicure before your due date. I was staring at my toes wishing I had.

8.) Send your modesty packing. You can assume your body is an open book the second you enter the hospital. This sounded awful when someone told the same thing. But I assure you, you won't think twice about it once contractions start.

9.) Eat. I repeat, eat. Eat something before you go to the hospital even if you aren't hungry. You will be 15 hours into labor and then it's too late. I learned this the hard way, begging for a saltine on hour 16, 17, and 18, getting denied every time.

10.) Don't wear nice lingerie. My bra had to be cut off in order to get the epidural wires in the right place and your underwear? Let's just say there is no reason to keep it.

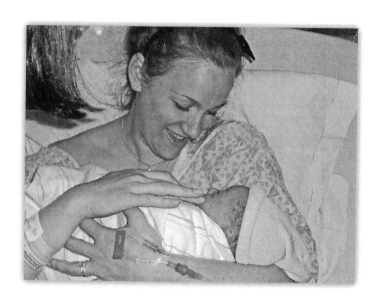

chapter two

TALES FROM THE BOOB

chapter two

PART I - Desperation

Breastfeeding Day 4, 9:00AM
Home from the hospital. Wish I could have tucked that lactation consultant in my pocket and brought her with me.
They don't tell you that your nipple is going to often erupt like Old Faithful spraying your baby in the face in all directions. You seriously spring a leak. I thought my nipple had popped open for God's sake. My child is trying to catch the geyser in her mouth by sticking out her tongue, hoping something will land inside.

Breastfeeding Night 4, 11:00PM
What the hell is this child's name again and why can't I think of it? Didn't I name her?

Breastfeeding Day 5, 7AM
I think my nipples just screamed. "Why are you allowing this Barracuda to naw on us?"

Breastfeeding Day 6, 4AM
Wait, so men can't breastfeed? Crap.

Breastfeeding Day 7, 10AM
Things you can do successfully with one hand while breastfeeding: NOTHING

Breastfeeding Night / Day 8, 3AM
Is that seriously another poop I just heard? How does something so small make so much shit?

Breastfeeding Day 9, 4PM
Walking around the house with no shirt on. Figured it was easy access to the milk truck that I have become.

Breastfeeding Night/Day 10, 2AM
Slept for 30 minutes. Had a dream that President Obama gave me a root canal.

Breastfeeding Day 11, 12:00PM
I feel like a drained well

Breastfeeding Night/Day 12, 3:35AM
Did I give birth to a boy or a girl? I forgot.

Breastfeeding Day 12, 4:25PM
Thank God we don't own cats. They would lick me up and down day and night because I'm covered in milk. I'm now picturing 10 cats licking every inch of my body and wanting to shower. But can't. Because I'm ... you guessed it, breast-feeding.

Breastfeeding Night/Day 13, 1:32AM
Maybe I'll write a book about what goes through your mind at 1am, 3am, and 4am feedings.

Breastfeeding Day 14, 10:45AM
I'M STARVING. The chips are so close yet so far...what happens if I just move a little bit to the right to...OUCH! Okay, no chips.

PART II - Delirium

Breastfeeding Night 15, 9PM
I need a chin strap. My neck is killing me from staring down at this child. A chin strap would be nice. I could deck it out in all sorts of fun colors and switch it up depending on what sweatpants I was wearing that day. I could open my own store and scream out the door to get mom's attention "Chin Straps & Sweatpants! Come get your chin straps and matching sweatpants!"

Breastfeeding Night 15, 9:30PM
Still on the same feed, a half an hour later. I think a breastfeeding feed bag is a better idea.
A chin strap/feed bag combo! I'm on to something. My hands are tied so if I could just dip my head down into a bag of potato chips and then pick it up and have it cradled while I chew... Brilliant.

Breastfeeding Day 16, 10AM
Something I'll never understand: Fishing. Also Daytime TV stinks.

Breastfeeding Night/Day 17, 2:40AM
I will not drop this baby. I will not drop this baby. I will not drop this baby.

Breastfeeding Night/Day 17, 4:10AM – 5:10AM
Slept. Had a dream I gave birth to a boy instead of a girl. The boy had testicles sticking out of his stomach. I went to go change him and started screaming for my husband because I didn't know how "boy parts" worked.

Breastfeeding Day 18, 3PM
You know those little crocodiles that bite something and don't let go no matter how much you shake them around? The term "motorboating" has a whole new meaning for me.

Breastfeeding Day 19, 8AM
Husband at work. So thirsty. Parched. Breastfeeding and can't get up. Help! I'm Breastfeeding and can't get up! Thinking about drinking my own breast milk. Is that wrong?

Breastfeeding Night/Day 20, 3:20AM
This is a form of torture in warfare. Letting you get 20 minutes of sleep and waking you up. I am being tortured. My whole body itches with tiredness.

Breastfeeding Day 21, 11:59AM
Hell is when your learning-how-to-eat baby misses your nipple

and starts sucking your areola. Have fun explaining the new hickey on your right breast to your husband.

Breastfeeding Day 22, 7AM
Finally figured out the pump yesterday. Or so I thought when I went to use it this morning and put the suction on the wrong part of my boob. If Hell is having your baby mislatch than Purgatory is having the pump suck up your areola instead of your nipple. Can you say "Boob Indian Burn?"

Breastfeeding Day 22, 9PM
Hubby's friend stopped by to visit the baby an hour ago. I forgot I wasn't wearing any bra pads and leaked through my shirt. I quickly grabbed my water and pretended to spill all over myself. Let's just say I'm not winning any awards for acting.

PART III - Resistance

Breastfeeding Night/Day 23, 1:50AM
Slept. Had a dream that I needed to breastfeed a rooster in order to keep it alive. Was very scared of beak.

Breastfeeding Day 24, 2PM
People keep asking me if I fall asleep while breastfeeding. Um, no people, I have a PIRANHA attached to the most sensitive part of my body at all times. No, I have not fallen asleep while breastfeeding.

Breastfeeding Day 24, 4PM
How cool would it be if they made a contraption like the ones the hot dog vendors have at ballparks for breastfed babies. I could just walk around the house all day with that thing around my neck and have her hoisted sideways at my boob. Hands-free breastfeed. Brilliant.

Breastfeeding Day 25, 10AM
I think I'll start mooing.

Breastfeeding Day 25, 10:30AM
Speaking of moo'ing - the couch used to be brown. With all of these new white spots it resembles a cow. I could moo to the couch and maybe it will start moo'ing back. It would be less quiet around here (see aforementioned comment about unwatchable daytime tv)

Breastfeeding Night/Day 26, 5AM
What if they gave awards for Breastfeeding? "Best Football Hold" "Best Squirted Nipple" "Best Letdown" "Best Use of Pump" "Least Likely to Drop Baby" "Biggest Areola"

Breastfeeding Day 27, 2PM
God I would love a manicure. Why don't nail salons' have outdoor spaces? On nice days people can sit outside while your baby sleeps in the car seat... and sip wine... yummm... wine...

Breastfeeding Day 27, 2:01PM
I really want a glass of wine.

Breastfeeding Night/Day 28, 3:33AM
Slept. Dreamt that my husband was actually our baby but had a grown-up voice and was talking and making uncomfortable jokes at a party. Woke up and fell back asleep - had a dream that my mother-in-law still pumped breastmilk and mixed it into her cat's food.

Breastfeeding Day 28, 9:45AM
Pumped breastmilk is liquid gold. Losing 1 ounce of pumped breastmilk by a mis-pour will reduce you to tears. In fact it just has.

Breastfeeding Day 28, 8:30PM
So I bought "Milkscreen" which tests for alcohol in breastmilk. You put a little on the strip and wait 2 minutes for your verdict. It's like the black screen of death when that thing comes back negative. It literally turns totally black after one glass of wine. I think not knowing might be better. Ignorance is bliss. Let me go back to that. I just want one glass of wine people!

PART IV - The Turning Point

Breastfeeding Night 29, 10PM
Why do I keep having 20 minute dreams about the President of the United States of America?

Breastfeeding Day 30, 1:30PM
Riddle me this: 2 hands, 2 boobs, 2 outlets on the pump plus one on/off switch. How the hell do you turn the pump on, with your toes? You laugh but I have actually tried this. I have literally attempted to turn the pump off with my foot while awkwardly holding the 2 apparatus's over my boobs. Any dignity left after childbirth it is now officially gone.

Breastfeeding Day 31, 5:30AM
She slept for 4 hours straight. Great news! Except now my breasts are so engorged I can't find the nipple. It's like one giant skin balloon.

Breastfeeding Day 32, 12PM
Saturday and going to Nana's house. Who knew a breast pump would be your latest accessory? I just convinced myself it looks like a new handbag.

Breastfeeding Night 33, 7:30PM
My God, look at these tiny hands and feet. I made this little person.

Breastfeeding Night 33, 10PM
The back of my neck is killing me from staring down at this tiny miracle. I can't take my eyes of her when she is feeding. I am memorizing her delicate little features.

Breastfeeding Day 34, 6:30AM
This little girl is so intent on getting nourishment. She is getting so good at eating. I'm actually proud of her.

Breastfeeding Night/Day 35, 3AM

The human body is amazing. The fact that my body is producing food and her body is consuming and staying alive by it... I am amazed.

Breastfeeding Day 35, 10:59AM
Have boob. Will Travel. My own portable feeding solution. And at least I don't have to steam clean, right?

Breastfeeding Night 36, 11:42PM
Slept for 2 hours. Had a dream that my little baby girl rolled over towards me, breastfed, and got up and walked away.

Breastfeeding Day 37
I never leave the couch but I still feel like I have this cool super power. Like I'm my own couch-super-hero.

Breastfeeding Night/Day 37, 3:20AM
It's almost like my daughter has two sides - the side that everyone sees and the private side when it's just her and me breastfeeding. She is at her most vulnerable, human level. It's hard to explain but I feel blessed to get to witness it. Even if it happens between 3 and 4am. I could get used to it.

PART V - Victory

Breastfeeding Day 38, 5:00AM
Where did these feel-good emotions come from? They are pouring out of me along with the milk!

Breastfeeding Day 38, 12PM
I want to stay like this forever - never go back to work, never go back to exercise, never go back to normal life... just stay right like this staring down at my creation. Keeping her alive on breastmilk.

Breastfeeding Day 39, 10AM
Milky mouth smiles are my favorite. I will never tire of seeing this child smile with a full mouth of milk.

Breastfeeding Night/Day 40, 1:45AM
I want to shower this child with milk love.

Breastfeeding Day 41, 3PM
I am a milk goddess. Hear me roar.

chapter three

TALES FROM THE COUCH

chapter three

After I delivered I never left the couch. Visitors would come and chat and I seriously never budged from my little spot on out brown couch with Little Miss. It felt safe there. I kept a running tally of "to-do's" and "not to-do's" during these visits.

Top 10 Rules for Visiting a 1st Time Mom Post Delivery:

1. Don't stay too long. An hour tops.
   Mommy's Thinking: *"What if they stay and I have to breastfeed? What if they want me to feed them? What if I fall asleep while their talking?!"*

2. Don't ask when they are going back to work. They do not want to think about this.
   Mommy's Thinking: *"I want to cry at the thought of leaving my baby to go to the bathroom so getting up, dressed, and out the door is not something I can process right now."*

3. Bring food. Without quesiton.
   Mommy's Thinking: *"I never remember to eat because I am trying to keep an infant alive and I'm starving. Please feed the animals."*

4. Heat up the food that you bring over, and put it on the plate.
   Mommy's Thinking: *"Okay, okay this is asking for too much but it would be so nice if I really never had to leave this couch."*

5. If she is wearing a "Hooter Hider" apron while breast feeding

do not pull it back to look at the baby. She is wearing it for a reason. (Yes, this happened to me.)

6. Let her see you wash your hands before you touch her newborn baby
    Mommy's Thinking: *"Did they take the subway here? Filth! Did they go to the bathroom before they came? Ew! Did they touch our elevator buttons on the way up? Gross!"*

7. Tell her she looks fantastic for just going through one of the most traumatic experiences in life.
    Mommy's Thinking: *"They haven't commented on how I look so I must look terrible. Validate me by acknowledging how hard labor is."* Hint: You probably do look terrible. But it's nice to hear a little white lie.

8. Bring a gossip magazine over.
    Mommy's Thinking: *"I would love to take my mind off keeping an infant alive for 10 minutes while she sleeps."*

9. Don't offer to babysit. It's too soon. I know people think this is a nice gesture and they are only trying to be helpful... but every time someone suggested this my heart wanted to rip out of my chest. It's irrational and emotional but picturing leaving your baby in someone else's care right after you give birth is very hard to do.

10. Tell her that her baby is beautiful and looks just like her even if they are covered in baby acne, slightly orange, and sport a receding hairline like your 70 year old uncle. *Sorry Little Miss but it was true...*

chapter four

TABOO TALES

chapter four

5 Things People Never Talk About Post Childbirth

1. Belly Jiggle. Not the "I ate too much Thanksgiving Dinner jiggle." Your stomach actually feels and looks like Jello. And not the little mini to-go cups of Jello; I'm talking a whole bundt cake of Jello.
Advice? Do not touch it, do not look at it. Ignore it, it's not the real you.

2. Night Sweats. You sweat for weeks after you give birth. I am talking a t-shirt change twice in any given night because you've soaked through it sweating. It's normal but no one told me about it and I thought I was dying.
Advice? Keep a t-shirt change next to your bed and wash your face first thing in the morning.

3. Sadness. You are sad. Really, really sad. And it's okay to be. These are not your true feelings; it is chemical. The problem comes when everyone around you is so happy; you feel like you ought to be too.
I like to take the opportunity to tell every new mom that this is normal and okay every chance I'm given. People only talk about how amazing it is to have children because a.) IT IS and b.) they forget about the first couple of weeks. Whenever a friend has a new baby I vow never to say the following: "Isn't it the best!?" "Aren't you so happy?" Because more often than not it isn't and you aren't. Not yet. If this happens to you I promise it will get better. Amazingly better.
Advice? Hang in there.

4. Exhaustion. People always told me "prepare to never sleep

again." I never believed them. I went into it so cocky thinking that other babies don't sleep but mine will. They don't. You run into people that say "MY baby slept 12 hours at a time at 8 weeks old, no problem." You will want to hurt these people. I had a mommy friend that told me this once. She followed that up by saying "Yeah, it's great, I only feed him at 11pm and 2am!" Um, sorry girlfriend, that is not a stretch of 12 hours. Check your math.

Advice? Nap when your baby naps whenever you can. (PS: I never followed this advice; wish I had.)

5. Delivery. I'm talking about the pushing and the breathing and the contractions, and the... you get it. I was told the following several times by several people: "You do yoga? You'll be fine! It's no problem because you're in great shape! That baby will shoot right out of you!" So of course I went in thinking I'd give birth within the hour and wouldn't feel a thing. Especially because I was a huge fan of my now new best friend called Mr. Epidural.

Reality Check #1: Little Miss took 21 hours to deliver. Every time the Doctor came in and said I'll check back in 5 or 6 hours my heart sunk. I could not believe I was still laying there with no baby after hour THREE.

Reality Check #2: The epidural numbness is only effective down to your spine which covers contractions but not so much the baby coming out part.

Advice? Go into the delivery room expecting to give birth to a MACK truck out of your ass and let's hope you are pleasantly surprised.

chapter five

TALES FROM THE OTHER SIDE

chapter five

I stand corrected. Here are three examples of how your brain changes after you become pregnant and give birth.

#1. I used to think kid's artwork was pretty horrible. Don't get me wrong I would play along and tell the parent how cute it was, blah blah. But in my head I was thinking it looked like the kid swallowed glue and glitter and threw it up on a piece of construction paper.

And then it happened: I was handed Little Miss' first piece of artwork she did at daycare. My heart melted. It was the most beautiful art I had ever seen. I couldn't stop staring at it. I kept picturing her with a big smile on her face enjoying this new feeling of (kid-friendly, non-toxic) paint on her hands and the freedom to put it wherever she pleased. I could her fun and joy in each smear. I loved knowing she had this new experience. It represented her first little act of independence.

#2. I used to be annoyed by ultrasound pictures. Pre-Little Miss I would go over to people's homes that were expecting and see that stupid ultrasound picture up on the refrigerator. I thought this was really dumb. Why the hell would you display a picture if you can't tell butt from head?

And then it happened: I got my first ultrasound picture. I was so damn proud of that thing. I cut them out and mailed them to my entire family. I brought one to work to show my co-workers. I even put one (yup, you guessed it) right on the fridge. I would make cheesy comments to my husband like "ohhhh she has your nose or ohhhh would you look at that I think she has my hands."

#3. I'm just gonna go ahead and put this one out there. I liked the smell of my daughters poop. Like, not only didn't mind it but actually liked it. It smelled like buttered popcorn. Don't knock it until you try it. Mark my words: Your own baby's poop does not smell bad.

chapter six

TALES FROM BEHIND THE STIRRUPS: The Post Birth Check-Up

chapter six

The dreaded post birth check up.

No one ever talks about the mandatory 6-week Doctor appointment post birth. I can't speak for those who had a C-section but if a MACK truck came ripping out of your ass like it did mine, then this tale is for you.

I was so excited to see the Doctor that delivered my baby. You go through. You want to thank them with every fiber of your being. But then 6 weeks later she asks you to lay back and open your legs.

I tried, I really did. My legs were locked shut. It was being in that room, in that position, with the same Doctor that ripped a baby out of me... it all came flooding back. She tried to coax me through it. She had me take deep breaths. We visualized sitting in a grassy pasture with cool wind in my hair and sun on my face. Nothing worked. I was having an all out panic attack and my legs would not respond. She resorted to prying them open with her hands. She literally had to get up on that little step and put her whole body weight into spreading my knees apart.

Once they were down they began to shake so badly she had to wait a whole five minutes to do anything. Five minutes is an eternity when you are in that position. Doc then assures me that the speculum is no bigger than the average penis. She is holding up her pinky. I thought she was kidding but right when I started to laugh I realized she had a serious expression on her face. Poor woman.

After the ordeal is done I sit back up for the verdict. And it's one that you never, ever want to hear: "Everything is

functioning fine but there is one thing you should know....you have a floppy vagina."
Dear, God.

Tip: In case you ever find yourself in a similar situation, the treatment for F.V. syndrome (I just made that up so don't Google it) is Kegel exercises. And you do return to normal, I promise.

chapter seven

TALES FROM THE CRIB

chapter seven

Tip: Don't ever ask another new mom how long their kid sleeps through the night in the event it's longer than yours. A) She's probably lying, and B) you'll want to cause physical harm.

This is pay back for all of the years I never slept as a child. Let me tell ya, pay back's a bitch.

Little Miss is 9 months. I've outlined her sleep timeline:

0-2 months: The Dance
I swear she is teasing me. I put her in her crib after nursing and she falls asleep immediately. I stagger over to the guest bed and lay down eager to clock the 2 hours of sleep before the next feeding. Right as I drift off her eyes pop open. I can hear them. Most mornings we are so exhausted from this song and dance that I resort to bringing her into bed with me.

2-4 months: Goats & Pigs

I embrace the swaddle I initially fought so hard against. God Forbid I ever hinder my babies freedom or imagination. If she wants her arms straight up in the air while she sleeps than darn it I wouldn't be the one to stop her! And then I get over myself. I'm swaddling the crap out of her and it works. But now she is making weird farm animal noises all night and I still don't sleep.

4-6 months: The Michelin Man

She keeps kicking out of her swaddle. Do you know how hard it is to re-swaddle when you are half awake at 3am? I need something else, she won't sleep without it. Enter the most amazing baby product ever invented since the pacifier: Baby Merlin's Magic Sleep Suit. The suit makes her feel swaddled but allows her arms and legs to be free. Thank you, Merlin. I wake up in a panic because she actually sleeps more than 4 hours. Oh, Irony.

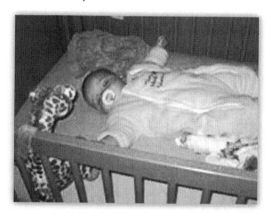

6-9 months: Practice, Practice, Practice

What's that Little Miss? You can roll over and crawl and talk to yourself now so why waste time sleeping? Right. Got it. Back to Square One. She is so tired after an hour of practicing said skills that I find her sitting up in the crib, head against the bumper, passed out. That's right... my baby now sleeps sitting up.

Our daycare got a picture of this and thought it was so funny they "framed" it.

Other Tips To Try Getting Your Anti-Sleep Baby To Sleep:

1. Use white noise,

2. Roll up two soft blankets and lay them on either side of your baby (only if they are swaddled and can't get tangled in them). They may like resting their cheek on it.

3. Introduce a "Lovee." Even if they have no interest in it at first, keep it around during calm-down time. They will eventually get that it signals rest and it will become a life saver.

4. Get an exercise ball. Hold your swaddled baby and bounce up and down gently on the ball. Works as well as the car and saves you the gas.

chapter eight

TALES INVOLVING A COMPETITIVE MOMMY

(err... Bitch)

chapter eight

Hubby and I brought Little Miss to the Science Museum on Sunday. They have a great infant room where kids under the age of 12 months can play. There was one other couple there with a boy just about Little Miss' age. Hubs and I really enjoy watching Little Miss do her thing in a new environment. She's such a curious little creature; I love that about her. The little boy comes crawling over to Little Miss and starts to play with the ball she had. I think the social interaction of two infants is really cool, I could just sit there and observe it all day. Enter the buzz kill (Competitive Mommy = CM): "No, No you can't take that ball away from her she has that ball now." I reply as a way to ease any awkwardness: "Oh, it's okay they don't know the difference they are just playing, it's all good." CM proceeds to yank her kid away from my daughter and says in the most annoying of teacher-voices: "It doesn't matter if they don't KNOW you still have to teach them right from wrong." I was so taken aback that words just started spilling out of my mouth..."Oh, Ok, well, she is used to this she is in daycare 3 days a week so kids take toys back and forth all the time" Officially changing CM to CB.

CB: "Isn't that sad if that is what they are teaching her in daycare."
I looked at my husband.
I looked back at her.
I looked at her husband (who's head was now hanging in embarrassment).
I looked back at hubs. We both just started laughing. We ignore them and get back to enjoying our daughter. But CB would not stop. She was out for blood.

CB: "How old is she?"
Me: "9 months"
CB: "Exactly 9 months?"
Me: "Um...a little older I guess... probably 9.5 now."
CB: "But when was she born?"
Me: Are you KIDDING me? I don't play the weeks game. I stopped saying how many weeks old she was at 12. Partly because I find it super annoying and partly because I hate doing the math.
Me: "She was born on April 21st."

  Just my luck, "The First Boy Ever Birthed" was also born in April. I could practically see the competitive thought-bubbles popping out of her head.

  Little Miss starts to crawl back over to "The First Boy Ever Birthed" despite my efforts to distract her from this toxic family. The kid snatches her toy away. Little Miss looks at him with a furrowed brow like she was trying to figure out how to proceed.

CB: "Ohhh look honey she has stranger anxiety stuff going on so why don't we just back away from her slowly and give her space."

  She looks up at me and points to her kid... "HE doesn't have ANY stranger anxiety, he loooooooves people." Hubby has to kick me because I'm about to swing at her. They are getting up to leave and we've continued to ignore them. She is standing there staring at us. Little Miss is practicing standing up on a bookcase and accidentally hits her head. She gives a little wail so I scoop her up, kiss her head, and put her right back down with a smile. Little Miss is fine and resumes playing.

CB: "Wow, she gets more love from you then my son does. When he falls down I NEVER make a big deal out of it I let him cry and cry."
CB's Hubby (he speaks!!??): "Umm, No you don't."
Hah! Sorry 'bout it lady. There is no way this woman has any friends.

And because I can't help myself - your son's name is Theodore and you were in the Infant Room of the Boston Science Museum at 11:42am on Sunday, January 29th, 2012 and here's a little tip - There is no script for parenting. There is only a right way for *your* kid and only you know what that is. Be confident and stop judging others to make yourself feel better.

But I'll end this on a positive note...

I bought the children's book "Beautiful Oops" at the Science museum and am loving it. Each page celebrates simple mistakes like a coffee stain, a crumbled piece of paper or spilled paint by turning them into beautiful works of art. In a world that is obsessed with perfection and status I think this is a great message for our little ones.

chapter nine

TIPS, TALES, AND TOOLS

chapter nine

I'd like to share that I am literally eating baby food out of a jar right now. So please use your best judgement when deciding whether or not to take my advice.

Top Ten Tips & Tricks For New Moms

#10 Take An Early Parenting Class (0-3 months)

Isolation, Fear, Guilt, Sadness. Welcome to my book! Just kidding. These are some of the negative feelings that may come up after childbirth. If you felt like you were the only person in the Universe to have just given birth then go take an early Parenting class. For Mass. residents, go to Isis and register for the Great Beginnings class. I must admit I went into this class thinking it wasn't for me but upon advice of a good friend I went anyway. I came out on the other side of it with boosted confidence and a group of girlfriends that will be in my life for a long time. We discussed it all, no holds barred. It was the therapy I needed at a time when I would never admit that I needed therapy.

#9 "Nurse With Confidence" (Start of Breastfeeding to End)

Buy Milkscreen. You have to laugh at their attempt at marketing. Even the box is sterile and medicinal. If it were up to me I would go the complete opposite route and promote the crap out of the fact that it tells you whether or not you are too drunk to nurse your baby. "Mommy's Night Out! Go Get Hammered!" But seriously, I probably should have bought stock in this company.

The results are annoying though. I would have a beer and a half on an empty stomach and the strip would come back negative and then I'd have to dip into the golden supply of pumped milk (Oh, the horror). Ref: TALES FROM THE BOOB.

#8 Control The Clutter (Bottle Feeding to Solids)
   Now that I'm no longer nursing (I tapped out once the first tooth popped through) I often feel like my nights are consumed with washing bottles and accessories. To avoid making your counter top look like a plastic factory,

#7 Get The Crud Out (0-3 Months)
   Here's something you might not know about chubby newborns: They get nasty old milk stuck in their skin folds. Yup, just like a bulldog. Use the cheap Target brand washcloths to get the nasties out. Cheap as heck and works like a charm.

#6 Treat Your Baby Like A Vampire (0-6 months)
   I was due in the Spring. Everyone told me how lucky I was because the weather would be nice. Not so much. (PS, Who knew that you couldn't use sunscreen on your baby until 6 months??)
   You will do everything you can to avoid exposing your baby's skin to the sun. It is a constant problem. UppaBaby makes a miracle sun canopy for any infant seat that allowed me to take Little Miss out for a walk sans-guilt.

#5 Back The F Up
   There will come a point when you run out of things to do with your child in your home. The walls will cave in on you. You will have played with every toy, read every book, sung every song, and peek-a-boo becomes old hat. When this happens to you, go buy a bunch of balls, put them in a playard, and then let your baby play independently. What? Independently?? Yes. Back away from your kid and teach them how to play on their own.

#4 Pretend You Spent A Lot On Your Diaper Bag...Then Don't
   I was so against spending over $100 to carry something that would carry something that would eventually carry my daughters shit in it. I get compliments on this bag everywhere I

go. People don't even really believe it's a diaper bag. (Sidenote: A friend of mine is a prominent personal stylist in Boston...after I bought this bag I saw that she had the same one. Nailed it.)

#3 Cut Your Baby's Nails Drunk
    I'm joking. Kind of. I drink a beer before I cut Little Miss' nails. That's actually not true I drink two beers. It's just enough to get me over my fear of doing it. It gives me the confidence to get in there and get it done. Go ahead and judge but for the record, I have drawn blood o times after taking this approach.

#2 Suck It Up. Literally.
    Your baby will get sick at least 9 times in the first year. That is a lot of mucus, my friends. Enter the snot sucker, named Nose Frieda. This thing is bad ass. Yes, you SUCK the snot out of your baby's nose (without it reaching your lips). This tool is so much more thorough than a traditional aspirator. And yes, I realize the ridiculousness of using the term "thoroughness" when it comes to snot sucking. If this is not love I do not know what is.

And.....The #1 Tip (This One's For The Guys)
What Not To Say To Your Wife After She Bears Your Child...

ME: (looking at self sideways in the mirror): "Ew, what they say about pancake boobs after nursing is true. I am totally getting a breast lift when we are done having kids."

Hubby: "I will totally pay for that."

chapter ten

TALES FROM THE EMERGENCY ROOM

chapter ten

I brought Little Miss to our yoga studio so I could get some odds and ends done, thinking it was the perfect place for her to explore. I mean it's one big room what could go wrong?

I was taking down a bulletin board in the front desk area and I noticed she was at my feet. I looked down and saw that she was making these weird chewing noises while coughing. My heart sunk. I convinced myself a tack fell off the bulletin board onto the floor and it was now wreaking havoc on my poor baby's esophagus. Total panic sets in. I reach into her mouth and dig around. She starts to bawl. I throw her in the car seat and rush her to Mass General.

She's happy as a clam by the time I get there but all I can see in my mind is a metal thumb tack poking tiny holes in her stomach lining. I want to throw up. They take her vitals and I'm trying to keep it together. Hubby shows up and I lose it. I'm the worst mother of all time; I let my baby swallow a push pin for Christ's sake.

One hour later they are taking an X-Ray of her little chest. Little Miss is obsessed with the machine and loving every minute of it. The Resident and the Attending come in 30 minutes after that and I can't help but sense they are hiding smiles. The Attending says to me, "So you let your baby hang out with razor blades and thumb tacks, huh?" My heart sinks for the second time.

She is kidding. She holds my head in her hands and assures me everything is okay, nothing was picked up on the

X-Ray, and not to worry. I want to hug her and take her out for a beer. But instead I thank her and we head home. Nice little Friday we had.

Meanwhile, my husband says to me:
"You've got some weird stuff going on in your brain. There's like this little man in the back of your head whispering things and pulling strings. I probably have a little man in the back of my head too but at least I beat the shit of him."

chapter eleven

TALES FROM THE BOXING RING

chapter eleven

I love my daughter more than anything in this world. And she loves me back. Really, really, REALLY hard.

Ways in which I get beaten up by a 10 month old

She rips the hair out of my head.
Sometimes we'll take her into our bed if it's before 6am and we aren't ready to get up. She lays in between us looking sweet as an angel, but then it begins. She starts to grab my hair and pull it out of my head, strand by strand. I try to stop her but she's relentless. It's like her own little meditation procedure. Instead of prayer beads, it's my hair. I try to nudge her towards hubby to see if she'll do it to him instead of me. I'm a really nice wife. She starts yanking at his hair and he smiles; says he likes it. Men. She soon discovers his hair isn't very long though, gets bored, and turns back to torture me.
Pain Meter: Hair-raising

She head-butts.
Little Miss will tilt her head all the way back and then BULLDOZE it into your forehead. The look of confusion on her face that follows is pretty entertaining. But the bruises on her head are horrifying. Hubby insists on explaining to every doctor we see that she's really into head-butting lately and that it must be a stage. I tell him he sounds like he is overcompensating and they are going to think we beat the poor kid. He shuts up immediately. Mom tells me this is Little Miss' 10-month-old-way of establishing her dominance. I'll take it.
Pain Meter: Headache producing

She sticks her finger up my nose.
　　I haven't had a bloody nose since grade school. I've had two in the last month. Little Miss thinks this is hysterical and jabs her finger so hard up my nose that it feels bruised for days.
Pain Meter: Reduced to Tears

She kicks me in the gut.
　　Fact: Little Miss hates getting dressed. Hubby is hoping she gets over this by the time she's a teenager. When I lay her on the bed and try to put clothes over her head she fights me like crazy. She recently discovered that kicking me in the stomach causes me to jump back hence stopping the dressing process. So she does it over and over and over again.
Pain Meter: Minor, but Severly Annoying

She hits.
　　I'll admit it, I kinda like this one. If she hasn't seen me all day and I through the door, she gets so excited. I scoop her up and she starts smacking my face with both hands, huge smile across her face.
Pain Meter: Worth It.

chapter twelve

TALES FROM A DISGRUNTLED MAMA

chapter twelve

PET PEEVE; NOUN A PARTICULAR AND OFTEN CONTINUAL ANNOYANCE; PERSONAL BUGBEAR

Top 5

1. The jelly roll that I now call my stomach. It just Won't. Go. Away. It doesn't matter what I do. I have an elliptical in my bedroom and actually use it. I do sit-ups every night. For Christ's sake I OWN a yoga studio. That jiggle is not budging. I'm considering sending out address cards. "We've Moved! John and Jane Jiggle are so excited to announce their new permanent residence at Kristin's midsection. Come by and see us!"

2. The abundance of Dennison's that come with everything you'll ever buy for your child.
    Oh, you don't know what a Dennison is? Neither did I. And then I got so annoyed by them that I had to look it up. Go ahead, I'll wait.
    Let this be a warning, if you buy anything kid related there are like 90 of these suckers attached to any damn product. Yes, a minor annoyance. Except when you miss one and it ends up in your daughters sock and she screams bloody murder because something is poking at her foot.

3. Baby/Toddler Clothing. What the hell is up? It's like the clothing companies got together and decided they were going to make sizes that would fit either baby midgets or Frank the Tank. Here is a picture of 2 pairs of LM's pants, each a different brand but BOTH sized 12 months:

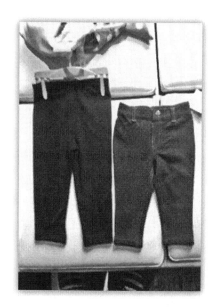

4. The statement: "Apple doesn't fall far from the tree" after having a child. Don't ever let these words fall out of your mouth to a new mom unless their baby just did a triple Salchow on ice skates while reciting the alphabet backwards.

5. Toys that randomly play music even after you hit off. This is just plain creepy. I once had a nightmare where a Teddy Bear was screaming "HUG ME, LOVE ME" while holding a tea pot that was singing "TIME TO SHARE A SPOT OF TEA! ONE FOR YOU, ONE FOR ME!" All the while the Teddy Bear was trying to dodge a bowling ball that shrieked "ROW ROW ROW YOUR BOAT GENTLY AS CAN BE! ONCE YOU SPIN ROUND AND ROUND ITS FUN AS FUN CAN BE!"

    I need therapy.

chapter thirteen

TALES FROM THE CONFESSIONAL

chapter thirteen

  A couple of days before I gave birth, I remember asking my mother the following question: "Will I love my baby as soon as she comes out?"
  I will never forget her brutally honest response: "Probably not. They take a full day of your life away from you... sometimes longer... while you writhe in pain. And they come out screaming and bloody and slimy. It takes a little while but you will soon love her more than anything else in this world." I needed to hear that. All anyone ever talks about is the amazing parts. It's that same type of brutal honesty that I like to give back. So here it is, in black and white and a little slimy, My True Confessions, from pregnancy to Little Miss' 11th month of life.

• I had an all out melt down when I went to register for my baby shower. I stepped one foot inside the Babies R Us, took a look at the breast pump accessories, and fell apart. My sister had to compress me.

• I got a speeding ticket when I was 8 months pregnant (Sorry, Mom).

• Due to "Pregnancy Brain" at 9 months, I drove so far in the wrong direction home from work that I started seeing signs for Albany, NY. I work in Massachusetts. I really shouldn't be allowed to drive.

• I never got out of this bathrobe or these pajamas. My back was killing me, I was tired, bloated, and miserable. I wanted to hurt my husband for even having the camera out. It looks like I'm smiling but really I'm planning his demise. Stomachs should not be allowed to get this big.

• Directly after giving birth I would get weirdly jealous if I heard someone else was pregnant. I wanted to be the only person that had gone through the experience even if only for a little while.

• When I was nursing I would melt a block of muenster cheese and eat it straight off the plate. I'm lying, I still do this now.

• I buy pumpkin pie baby food with the intent of feeding it to Little Miss but end up eating it all myself.

• Sometimes I fake a really long shower. It's the only true me time I have. I love standing there with the water running over my head and staring at the wall. This may sound sad and pathetic but I love every minute of it so please don't feel bad for me, really.

• People on the street will mistake Little Miss for a little boy but I don't have the energy to correct them so I just pretend she is one. She can send me the therapy bills later.

• I enjoy getting the snot out of my daughter's nose.

• I am guilty of buying everything that Diapers.com recommends for me.

- I still haven't childproofed our condo.
- I still wear maternity jeans.

chapter fourteen

TALES FROM MY HEART:
Little Miss Turns 1

chapter fourteen

It's 10pm on April 20th, 2012. A year ago today I was sleeping in my bed on my left side per recoomendation of every maternity website (as if you aren't neurotic enough). 4 days overdue with what I would soon learn was my Little Miss. I'm nostalgic, and sad, and happy, all at once. I remember it like it was yesterday.

It's 12:05am and I am wide awake sitting straight up in bed. I think I have to take a big dump.

I walk sleepily to the bathroom but nothing happens. Hmm, weird. I get back into bed but something doesn't feel right. I get out of bed again and start pacing the bedroom. My husband starts to snore. I start damning all men in all the Universe. I want to be sleeping so deeply that I'm snoring. I haven't slept that deeply since I was 5 months pregnant. I would love to say that what followed was my yoga teachings kicked in, making me feel zen and ready to go. Not so much. I run to the bathroom again prepared for the biggest crap of my life. (When I relate this notion to my husband a few weeks later he deadpans "sexy").

Again, nothing. I grab my beloved bathrobe and wrap myself up. I start pacing the entire condo. I'm hungry. I open the refrigerator 4 times but can't find anything I want to eat. All of a sudden my lower belly seizes and lurches forward. I stumble. holy shit. HOLY. SHIT. Contraction ONE and I'm brought to my knees!? I did not sign up for this. It happens again. I run to the bathroom to throw up, multiple times. Hubby wakes up and comes over to rub my back. I want to be male.

I've had two contractions and I'm ready to give up (little did I know I had 21 more hours of this). We call the hospital in a panic. THIS HURTS GOD DAMN IT. Why does it hurt so soon? I thought it would be gradual? What happened to gradual!? I swear I am the only person ever to be in this amount of pain. The Doctor-On-Call tells me that he can hear me pacing and commands me to stop; he tells me I need to save my energy. My teeth start to grind as I try to stay still.

He asks me how far apart the contractions are and I answer about 12 minutes. I think I'm about to have a baby within the hour. He tries to convince me to stay home as long as possible because they will probably die down. Sam and I are in the car before he could get the words out.

It's 4am and no one is on the road. I've heard stories where couples driving to the hospital reminisce about their care-free DINK* lives and wonder how it would all be different soon. Not us. My mind is completely blank; a sheet of white pain seizing my body every 10 minutes. Hubby pulls into the wrong entrance and I see panic in his eyes for the first time. I think to myself there is no way I can go through with this. We find the right entrance and the guard asks me if I want a wheelchair. No way. No how. I will stll have my dignity even if I'm being ripped open.

I waddle into the waiting room and call my mom. I hear her sleepy voice and start to bawl. I want my mommy more than anything right now. She tells me how much she loves me and she'll be by my side in 10 minutes. She gets there in 9. I am about to find out how much a daughter means to a mother...

*DINK - "Dual Income, No Kids"

Little things about Little Miss that make my heart melt

Those two little curls that pop up over your ears.

How you cuddle into my chest right before you fall asleep.

When you kiss your dolls before bed and wave to them when you wake up.

The sound of your breath when you're in a deep sleep.

Those belly laughs.

That little bum.

When you're being mischievous.

Listening to you call "ya ya" when you look for me.

The determined look on your face when you're trying something new.

And that big open-mouth smile ever since you were born

You are the best thing I've ever done. You were worth every minute of pain.

Happy 1st Birthday Little Miss.

chapter fifteen

TALES FROM DAYCARE: Why Does This Sound Like My College Experience?

chapter fifteen

Little Miss P goes to a daycare in Boston called Bright Horizons. I know it sounds like the name of a rehab but they are very good and I highly recommend them. Teachers fill out "Infant Daily Sheets" that you get handed every time you pick your child up. They are amazing and I would be lost without them. They tell me how much she drank down to the ounce, how long she's slept, when she peed, pooped, and what the poop looked like.

I am a control freak and need this kind of attention to detail. At the bottom of the sheet they leave notes about her day. Insert "Kristin" instead of "P" here and it pretty much sums up my entire college experience:

- "P finished her drink in no time and then partied all morning."

- "P looked at herself in the mirror for hours today."

- "P loves the kitchen. She knows exactly where the snacks are located."

- "P had a little too much to drink and threw up on her pretty new shirt."

- "Oh no! P backed herself into a corner and couldn't get out!"

- "P showed off her pretty dress today by strutting around the room."

- P loves to groove to every type of music and did a belly

dance before lunch."

- "P had a blast when she discovered that she could do chin-ups on everything she sees."

- "P decided to drink, roll, and sleep today."

- "P did sit-ups in bed and then fell asleep sitting up."

- "P threw a neon green scarf in the air, did a dance with it, and then tried to shove the whole thing in her mouth. She should be in movies."

chapter sixteen

TALES FROM THE UNDERBELLY

chapter sixteen

It probably doesn't make sense to read this if you are pregnant.
Although I sure as hell wished someone had told me after delivery I'd be soaking in a Sitz bath, taking stool softener every hour and wearing enormous maxi pads in old lady underwear like an 8th grader, I probably wouldn't have listened anyway. I was too busy planning my playlist for the hospital and making sure I had cute post-delivery outfits packed. Little did I know I was about to have the least glamorous experience of my life.

5 things that surprised the crap out of me after giving birth:

1. Did you know you can't be moved from the delivery room to the postpartum room until you pee in front of the nurse? Oh yeah, you have to PROVE you can go. Let me tell you the last thing you feel like doing after giving birth to a MAC truck is getting up from bed, walking the 5 miles to the bathroom and then sitting down on a cold toilet in front of a nurse while she waits until you go. I felt like my insides might fall right down into the toilet. My pride already had.

2. Speaking of surprising the crap out of me: You'll most likely be backed up for a week dreading this. You'll probably Google it and see buzz words like "Perineum", "Bowel-Movement", and "Anal Cleansing." All of these words are horrifying and so is the first time you go. Just know that it will pass (pun completely intended). It's going to happen and the more you fight it, the worse you'll feel. Don't forget to take your stool softeners. So hot, right? Just seeing that bottle gives me the shivers.

3. You have to use a squirt bottle to clean yourself for 4 days after giving birth. A squirt bottle, people. I think I'll just let this one resonate.

4. The nurses will give you the most dreadful looking disposable underwear to wear in the hospital. It's like wrapping yourself in an ace bandage. You will look at them with sad eyes and wonder if you will ever get to wear your pretty little hanky pankies again. But you will miss these granny panties when you get home. They are just so convenient. (Bonus Tip: Steal as many as you can from the hospital).

5. You will soak in a sitz bath to feel "better" about your hemorrhoids, but really this will make you feel 100 and defeated. I remember having the nurse check me out Day 2 in the hospital. I rolled back over and she handed me this crazy contraption. I looked at her like she was equally crazy, "What is this for?" To which she replied, "Hemorrhoids." To which I replied "But I don't HAVE hemorrhoids." To which she replied, "Yes.... ya do." I watched as my pride sunk into a round pot for the second time.

For my preggo's that decided to read this entry anyway:

A year ago today I was four weeks postpartum celebrating Mother's Day by sitting on a doughnut pillow, getting my boobs gnawed on, and crying at every Tide commercial. This year I was greeted in the morning by an endearing 1 year old holding flowers showing me how to sniff them, a lively discussion using her three favorite words: ("apple", "dog", and "up"), and the most delicious nose kisses before bed. The hemorrhoids were totally worth it.

chapter seventeen

TALES FROM THE BOOB PART DEUX
"Excuse Me, But I Didn't Order The Pancakes."

chapter seventeen

Here we go, round two of discussing mammary glands. I don't think I've said those words since high school Biology class. In TALES FROM THE BOOB we went on a little trip from the start of nursing to the finish but we never discussed the aftermath. I loved nursing (I know it's annoying when people say that) but the aftermath is ugly. I've dubbed it "Breakfast Boob Syndrome."

Women told me about the pancake boob factor post-nursing but no way did I think that would apply to me. I just smiled and thought "not these ta-tas." My boobs were fun. They were full. They looked good under a shirt. They would do what they needed to do for my baby and go right back to where they started. Not so much. The skin on these puppies is not hot and not going away.

For example, if I pinched a section of my pre-nursed boobs I would be able to grab a nice chunk of fat. Fat full of life. Now when I pinch myself (what, you don't pinch your boobs?) all I get is sad, lackluster skin. No more fun. No more sunshine. My boobs need to go on depression meds. What's worse is that I walk around my house and see things that remind me of my deflated Breakfast Boobs daily.

Talk about Body Dysmorphic Disorder. I walked into a lingerie store to give my Breakfast Boobs a shot of caffeine and the woman there asked me what size I thought I was. With confidence I answered a 36C/D. She gave me a confused look and said "let's just check to make sure." She wrapped measuring tape around me, offered a crooked little smile and replied, "Look dear, you are a 32B/C." I felt like saying, "Yeah but what if I just pick them up like this and then smoosh them together like so... check again?!?!"

Anyone suddenly craving pancakes?

chapter eighteen

FROMUNDA TALES

chapter eighteen

You know how in movies when newborn babies come out of their mothers and look like beautiful cherubs with perfect features? Yea well those babies are actually 7 month old paid actors. And they are doing a disservice to new moms expecting to see the Gerber Baby emerge from their crotch. Newborns actually look like Gremlins. And after a couple of weeks it gets worse, not better. This surprised me. Because who talks about how nasty a baby is at first? I mean, why would you? Welcome to my blog.

Disclaimer:
While all of the below is real and happens, in a few months you will get that angelic baby, don't you worry.

THE NEWBORN NASTIES:

• Your newborn will probably get acne. Like worse than any adolescent you've seen. Worse than the images you see in Proactive commericals. You won't want to leave the house. You'll feel like you are the only one with a pimply baby. You will call your pediatrician. You will have nightmares of acne scarring on those sweet baby cheeks for weeks.

• Your newborn will have a black slash purple slash bloody belly button that will have its own zip code. You will pray for the day it falls off. And then it does and you will freak out. Because you will be left with this mass of nastiness and cells you don't know whether to frame or throw away.

• You will find "dust bunnies" of old lint in between their toes and fingers. Every single day if not every hour. It's actually kind of hard to stay on top of.

• Your newborn will have enough wax coming out of their ears you could start your own candle company; specializing in orange candles, of course.

• Your newborn will most likely get a condition called Cradle Cap* which I like to call Cradle Crap. Their heads will be covered in yellow scales that, if you are like me, you will sit around for hours and pick off.

*Extra bonus Cradle Crap tip: Wipe it with a little olive oil, let it sit, and then wash it off. Repeat every couple days.

• They will get milk in their neck folds that you won't discover until days later. Your baby will reek of curdled milk and you won't know why. Peel apart their skin folds and you'll discover the culprit.

• Your newborns fingernails will constantly have black dirt under them. Do you know what this is from? YOU. It's all of the dirt that you don't see on your own body that collects under their nails. Yummy.

• Poop. Everywhere. Under the balls. Over the balls. Inside vaginal folds. Up the back. Down the leg. You will not believe how much shit comes out of a newborn and where it can end up. Brace yourself.

• So there you have it: Acne, Bloody Belly Buttons, Earwax, Scaly Heads, Cheese Necks, Dirty Appendages and Feces. Good times.

chapter nineteen

TALES FROM THE PUMP

chapter nineteen

Using a pump to get milk out of your boobs is absolutely ridiculous. Think about it: You plug in a machine, put cones on top of your chest, and watch as a body part plummets into a plastic tunnel. And to top it all off (pun intended) milk comes flying out and drips into a bottle. And this is 2013.

I want to meet the woman that says she enjoys pumping. Tell me you've bonded with your breastpump and I'll give you a great referral to a psychologist. The only reason women do this is to keep the milk flowing. Supply and demand: The more we are milked, the more we provide. Just like a cow's utters. And what's hotter than a farm animal?

I remember being 4 weeks post delivery and only breastfeeding. No big deal here folks; just trying to keep an infant alive solely on my ability to breastfeed. Zero pressure. I was using this amazing product called "Milkies" and catching the overflow from one boob while Little Miss nursed the other boob. I would then store the 1 ounce of drips I collected in the fridge. After a day I would get to about 4 ounces. I was doing this because I was terrified of the machine that was sitting in my closet. It would whisper as I walked by, taunting me. You know the Sex and The City episode where Miranda walks by the man in the Hot Dog suit and he whispers "eat me" just to her? She ignores him at first and then finally gives in and confronts him? Well I had a similar relationship with my pump except it whispered "I'm not going away" and never turned me on sexually.

The time eventually came when I wanted freedom more than the Milking. I couldn't drip enough on the non-nursed boob to make a bottle anymore with my "Milkies" so I called my older sister on Skype to walk me through the pumping preparation. I called her back four times to make sure I had the right end of one piece going into the right end of another. Mom was with me and seeing how nervous I was suggested I have a couple sips of wine first. (God love her.) I chug a half glass and go into the bedroom with the Pump. I get all set up and put the two cones over my boobs. Shit. What part of my body should I use to turn ON the pump if both hands are grasping the plastic cones, pray tell? I give up and go back out to the living room to call Sis again. Mom laughs out loud. "Try holding the cones up with your forearm while you turn the Pump on with your other hand. Just make sure you don't turn it up too high or it will hurt." I reply with a "Hell NO." She sighs and suggests I try one boob at a time. Deal. I go back into the bedroom, head sunk low, wondering when the humiliation will stop and if I will ever be a normally functioning female again. I put one cone to breast, take a deep breath, and reach for the on switch. Oh God. I turn it a quarter of an inch to the right and the thing explodes with noise. I jump back and detach. Why is it yelling at me!? I try it again with my eyes closed and feel my entire boob lurch forward and retreat in a rhythmic sort of way. It sucked... literally and figuratively. I open one eye and look down. Um, who invited the Long Nipple Tribe to this party?

    You can expect your cute little dimes to turn into ugly half dollars inside those plastic cones, damn them all to hell. But at least I got to go to the grocery store with my own boobs tucked inside a nursing bra and not attached to my daughters lips, right? Yes freedom does have its price. And I hope pumping is something you come to terms with if you decide to nurse. Overtime it becomes old hat. I even started calling mine "Priscilla the Pump Mate"; not because we bonded but because we spent so much time together. I carried her everywhere I went (Yea, my pump was female, so what?). When I turned her on she would groan over and over again: "Feed Me Feed Me Feed Me" as the suction went in and out. In retrospect my pump went from an annoying whisper to yelling at me to a repetitive drone. Sounds like a bad marriage. Maybe you'll get more lucky and have a male Pump

Mate with a raspy voice coaxing you on with something like "This is so hot, This is so sexy, God you turn me on"... but then he'd be one lying son of a bitch.

Tips:

1. Buy Milkies to delay the inevitable.

2. Put your cones in the fridge for the day so you don't have to wash them after every pumping session.

3. If your frozen milk smells like blood don't be alarmed, it's normal.

4. If you pinch your boob, milk will come out. Not really a "tip" I realize but this shocked the hell out of me so I'm just warning you. (You might be asking yourself Why is she pinching her boob? To which I would like to reply "Why not?")

chapter twenty

TALES OF CONCEPTION

chapter twenty

We are moving in August and started to pack up some small boxes here and there. I was going through my jewelry drawer and found the pregnancy test that confirmed I was with child in 2010. Yes, I kept it. Yes, it had dried pee on it. Don't judge me. Finding it made me think back to the time when Hubby and I decided we wanted to have a baby. We told each other things like "whatever happens, happens" and "if it's meant to be, it's meant to be." We were all love peace and hair grease about it. But then it didn't happen the first month and that attitude got old, fast. Hubby and I tend to be competitive. And if you know anything about this type of person then you know they expect that the harder they work, the more they achieve. Let me tell you something if you don't already know it: you can't try harder at this and expect to "do better."

I turned into a pregnancy testing freak. I thought I would be the only Super Human that could tell she was pregnant the second after coitus. I would literally run into the bathroom to test my pee right after doing the nasty. I tested every morning regardless if I had sex the night before because apparently that's when your pee is the "strongest." (PS: Do you know how expensive pregnancy tests are? It's like the pregnancy stick companies know they've got you by the balls.) I was obsessed. Finally, after a shower one day, I tested and waited the grueling 3 minutes it takes for the test to come back positive or negative. And when the 2nd pink line ever so slowly started to (barely) appear my heart literally jumped out of my chest. My eyes strained to see it. I put that stick right up to my pupil to make sure I wasn't seeing things; didn't even care it was dripping with fresh pee.

I've heard stories where people do really cute, elaborate things to let their husbands know a baby is on the way. Things like wrapping the positive pregnancy stick in a pink and blue box with a pretty ribbon on it. Maybe they even wash the stick first. Or they offer to cook dinner but then serve nothing but baby carrots, baby peas, and baby corn; gazing up at their hubby's confused look with a little giggle, chin to shoulder.

Not me.

The second I saw the lightest-pink-line-ever-seen-by-the-human-eye, I ran out of the bathroom butt ass naked. I grabbed Hubby's head and pushed HIS pupil into the (still dripping) stick. I excitedly yell "AHHH!" "Does that look like a second pink line to you??" Hubby slowly removes the back of his head from my hand, squints his eyes and states: "There's still PEE on that thing."

Romantic, eh?

chapter twenty-one

TALES FROM THE CAR

chapter twenty-one

Little Miss does not like to be strapped in a carseat and driven around. In order to calm her down and actually get anything done I turn on her favorite music. At the moment that happens to be four CD's of sung Nursery Rhythms on rotation. Have you ever really listened to the words in Nursery Rhythms? Lately I've been analyzing the lyrics because I'm just that bored with them. It turns out they are mostly gruesome, depressing, or sexist.

Take your basic Jack and Jill. I never knew the second half to it. Jack has to wrap his head in vinegar and brown paper after falling down a hill. Can you imagine having to wrap your head in vinegar? Ew. Little Bo Peep lost her sheep and then found them but all of their tails had been cut off! And the sicko that did it then hung them up to dry just to throw it in her face. Speaking of losing tails, not only were the Three Blind Mice blind but in a shitty twist of fate the farmer's wife chops off their tails. Now they are blind AND tail-less? That's no life for a mouse. All Old Mother Hubbard's dog wants is a bone but the cupboard is bare and we never do find out if he gets one. Peter Peter Pumpkin Eater just pisses me off. He had a wife but couldn't keep her so he puts her in a pumpkin shell? Come on.

Poor Jack Be Nimble practically gets his balls burned jumping over a candle. Don't even get me started about Rock A Bye Baby. The dish in Hey Diddle Diddle is a thief, Humpty Dumpty will never be the same, Mary's lamb is a stalker, Georgie Porgie was a player, and Little Miss Muffet can't get a decent meal.

So now I know why I feel like I need to pop Prozac

every time I get out of the car.

There is one kids CD I am loving and it's Sesame Street's "All Time Favorites." There are some real oldie but goodies on there: "C is for Cookie," "Rubber Duckie," and "People In Your Neighborhood" to name a few. They bring me right back to my parent's four poster bed with a tray of breakfast and a glass of milk. The other day hubby and I went out for a glass of wine sans Little Miss. Driving home Grover's song "Monster in the Mirror" came on. Windows down, we cranked it up, screaming at the top of our lungs: "WOBBA WOBBA WOBBA AND A DOODLY DOO." The guys next to us in the Chevy waiting for the light were less than impressed.

chapter twenty-two

TALES FROM MY POTTY MOUTH: Why My Toddler Says Shit A Lot

chapter twenty-two

If you are used to swearing everyday it's very hard to switch this instinct off. I have the mouth of a trunk-driver. Sure, I scaled it back a bit when Little Miss was born but an occasional expletive still slips out here and there. I said the word shit twice in Little Miss' presence and it was just in time for her to become a verbal copy-cot.

The first time I let it slip I was in Target. She loves to ride in the shopping cart when we go grocery shopping. Target has these massive double seated cart options for moms with multiple kids. Little Miss spots this and insists she be put in it. We'll call it the B.A.C. (Big Ass Cart). She stomps her feet and points at it shaking her head yes so hard I think it's going to pop off. After about a minute of trying to persuade her to get into the normal sized carts I see her wedge herself under the B.A.C., belly down. F*ck it I think to myself and strap her in it. Mind you we are at Target to pick up one pack of diapers. Yes, 1 pack; an item that easily fits in one of those small little red baskets. Do you know how hard it is to push a B.A.C. with nothing in it to weigh it down? Plus it looks absolutely ridiculous pushing it completely empty. This is a picture of half of the B.A.C., I would have needed a wide ass lens to capture the second row of seats.

So with Little Miss smiling from ear to ear, off we go, slow as molasses. In order to make it to the baby section I had to turn the cart twice and with each turn put all of my weight into it. I literally stepped on the back bar and leaned my body into the handle bar. The thing has a turning radius of a truck. Not to mention it sounded like a rabbit in heat with all of the squeaking and moaning. After mistakenly missing the diaper aisle I tried to pull it back and turn it quickly but it was too late. Instead I did a pile drive into a free standing display of boxes. Naturally, I responded with a "SHIT!" and proceeded to pick up the kiddie potty's (never registering the irony of that until just now.)

The second time I let an expletive out of my mouth around Little Miss was when I had a full cup of water on the ottoman and spilled it all over the floor. I let out a quick "shit" under my breath and then did a quick glance over at her, hoping she didn't catch it. Little Miss looked at the water ... looked at me...looked back down at the water.... and what do you know but out comes a long drawn out "SHIIIIT" from my precious little 15 month old. And that's what it took for me to become the worst mother ever.

But now it's constant. If I even slightly bump into anything at all it's "Shit this" and "Shit that" from her mouth. She knows exactly when to say it and how to say it. She event points and gives a definitive nod when she does it. I'm totally screwed. People are starting to notice. The other day we were at a restaurant and the waiter spilled a little water on our table. Little Miss pointed at it and yelled "SHIT" while looking up at him innocently. I went into spin control while his chin touched his chest. "Yes honey that's right, he will *slip* if he's not careful." (I got a mouthed high five from hubby on that recovery). We went to the pediatrician recently and he asked how many words I thought she had. I turned bright red and replied "She says shit all the time, okay?" To which he burst out laughing and looked down at my daughter. And wouldn't you know with a big grin she nods and proudly says "Shit" right to his face. Still laughing he turns to me and says "Watch out with this one, you've got yourself a handful." Thanks Doc, that's really helpful.

Signed,
Mortified

chapter twenty-three

TALES FROM THE OB-GYN

chapter twenty-three

There will come a time when you just can't find a sitter and you have to go to your annual check-up. You will bring your baby with you to the OBGYN and hope to God she behaves. You will play 15 different games in the waiting room because your OBGYN is always late. When you resort to letting your child rip every page out of PARENTS magazine your name will finally be called and you will follow the nurse into the 10'x10' exam room. She will ask you to step on the scale and your toddler will scream bloody murder because she thinks you are about to be executed...

"Little Miss, everything is okay, Mama is just getting weighed! Look, it's SO fun!" All the while thinking holy shit if she thinks THIS looks scary wait until I'm lying prone with a floating talking head above my waist.

The nurse leaves and tells me it won't be long. 12 minutes later (2 hours in Toddler Time) I've let Little Miss have the run of the room. The OBGYN opens the door to the following scene: gloves strewn across the room, a white paper sheet originally covering the exam table ripped to confetti pieces, 2 stirrup covers draped over Little Miss' shoes, and her sitting on the floor eagerly flipping through a pamphlet on Spyhilis. (What? It had the most pictures.) The OBGYN stops in her tracks and whispers "Oh, My." Had she come in 5 minutes earlier she would have witnessed her cross-section uterus model getting violated by Elmo.

Have you ever noticed how eerily sensitive and perceptive children can be? Little Miss knew right away that this was not going to be a pleasant experience for me. She looks up at the OBGYN and immediately runs to me, gripping my legs. There was no way I could leave her loose in the room for this exam so I strap her in her stroller and wheel her up by my head.

When I put my feet up, her face breaks. She won't stop staring at the Doctor and the sheet over my knees. *Believe* me kid, this is worse for me than it is for you. I search my brain for a game I can play with the top half off my body. All I can think of is The Wheels On The Bus. If getting your privates examined isn't embarrassing enough let me tell you what doesn't help the situation: Swaying your forearms back and forth while singing "Swish Swish Swish" nine times, *all through the town.*

chapter twenty-four

baby ♡

TALES OF HYPOCRISY

chapter twenty-four
baby ♡

"People who live in glass houses should not throw stones."

Hello, my name is Mommy and I am a total hypocrite. Here is where I tell you all of the things I thought pre-pregnancy and/or pre-baby (hereafter known as PP&/B) and how all of that changed after getting pregnant and giving birth (AP&/B). To break the ice let me just begin by confessing that I do most of my thinking for this blog in the shower. Sometimes I run out of it butt naked and write down my thoughts; like just now.

PP&/B: I wanted to use a taser gun on Moms who used baby talk in public. You know that high pitched annoying voice that narrates everything the kid does? I used to buzz around the supermarket priding myself on getting all groceries in the cart within 30 minutes flat. Once in awhile I'd take a shortcut thru the baby aisle and get stuck behind a mother doing some sort of skit with her kid. "Oh YES Johnny those ARE the diapers you wear, GOOD FOR YOU. And yes they have kangaROOS on them and kangaROOS jump like THIS! (proceeds to jump like a jackass) HOP HOP HOP. Now can you go ahead and put them in the cart for Maaa-Maaaa?!" Hurl.

AP&B: I am now this deranged mother. Not just at the supermarket; everywhere we go. It's incessant and I can't stop myself. On Monday I was walking through the city around 10am, strolling Little Miss along the water. Right in the middle of me shouting: "Look Look, there are TWO birds, that's right TWO! Oh my and an AIRPLANE wayyyy up high. Can you stretch your arms WAYYY up high!?" I noticed a couple of guys in suits drinking coffee and discussing work. My annoying voice in juxtaposition to that adult conversation made me want to take a billy club to my own knees.

PP&/B: I told myself I would NEVER allow kid music in the car. My sister has 2 kids and every time we would visit their was always some obnoxious kid-song playing. Hubby and I would leave having full on discussions about how we would never allow this to happen. We loved our music too much. We would teach our dear baby how to love the likes of Aerosmith, Pearl Jam, Bob Marley, and Dave Matthews.

AP&/B: Not only do we have every toddler soundtrack under the sun, we rock out to it even when Little Miss isn't around. In fact, the other night right before I fell asleep I think I heard Hubby softly sing "Rain Rain Go Away" to put himself to sleep.

PP&/B: I watched a very pregnant woman have a glass of wine at a restaurant and proceeded to judge the living crap out of her with my eyes. I gave her the death stare and maybe even pointed once or twice.

AP&/B: Six months pregnant and I'm drinking a half a glass of wine every single Friday night until my due date. (And still ended up with a really smart kid. That just happens to love saying shit all the time.)
POT. KETTLE. BLACK.

PP&/B: I used to roll my eyes at women that were germ-a-phobic with their kids. Like, Jesus Christ lady it's a dollar bill not a syringe, why don't you buy him a bubble to live in while you're at it.

AP&/B: I am a sanitizing junkie. When Little Miss was an infant I bought a separate type of wipe for her butt, hands, nose, nails, bottles, and pacifiers all the while thinking they should make special baby sanitizing wipes for strollers and toys and cribs! Oh, my. I would greet people at the door with a bottle of hand sanitizer. When Hubby gently suggested this might be a little too forward I instead left it on the table, right in front of the couch. What I really wanted to do was put a big sign on it that read: "WHETHER YOU JUST WENT TO THE BATHROOM, TOUCHED MONEY OR BREATHED IN AIR PLEASE COAT YOUR HANDS IN THIS SHIT MULTIPLE TIMES AND LET ME WATCH YOU. THANKS, MANAGEMENT."

PP&/B: Whenever I saw a toddler throw a temper-tantrum in public I immediately thought the parents were total failures. Get a grip on your kid, would ya?

AP&/B: There is literally nothing you can do once your toddler throws herself into a downward spiraling tantrum. I'm reading this book where they suggest you mimic your child's frustration on her level. Like, bang your fists in the air, stomp your feet, scream "I want it now!" so she knows you understand where she is coming from. If not being able to control your child's fit isn't embarrassing enough, stooping to her level and faking your own tantrum certainly doesn't help the situation. Epic Fail.

PP&/B: God it was annoying when new parents got so excited about their own kid's small accomplishments. Awesome. Johnny peed on the pot. I'm so excited for you I could burst. Can we all go back to our lives now? Mary learned how to wave. I'm beside myself with glee. Want a cookie?

AP&/B: We threw a soiree when Little Miss learned that her sippy drink goes in the cup holder on her highchair. We took pictures with our phone and sent them to everyone we knew. We even called our parents on Skype to show them live what she was now a master at: sippy cup placement.
P.S. I think we've created a monster. Little Miss now claps for herself and shouts "Chob" for "Good Job" after every little thing she does. Oops.

PP&/B: I thought I would only MAKE all of my own

organic baby food. And I actually did this for about 2 months when Miss P was learning how to eat solid foods.

AP&/B: I peel her a banana and pat myself on the back.

And there you have it folks. Miss Judgy Judgerton herself ends up being the hypocrite. Now that it's off my chest I guess that makes my chest both figuratively and literally bare right now, given I am still naked writing this.

chapter twenty-five

TALES FROM A DERANGED SOCCER MOM

chapter twenty-five

I was a fairly competitive soccer player back in my day. So when I saw that Coco Baby in the South End of Boston was offering a soccer class for Toddlers I was all over it like white on rice. When Hubby found out the price of it his jaw hit the floor and he asked me to repeat it twice. I told him that when Little Miss eventually got a full ride to play soccer at Duke the cost would be totally worth it. And somehow that worked. Men.

The day before it started I was showing Little Miss my old uniform and trophies while practicing kicking a foam ball around her playroom. She didn't show much interest but I couldn't hold it against her; these were my glory days after all and most adults don't care when I casually mention I may have been a State Champion semi-finalist in 1997. Hubby always reminds me that this is not the same as winning.

It's 45 minutes before class and I'm waiting outside the door looking way too eager than anyone should about a toddler soccer program starring two dolls named Mimi and Pepe. So we take a little walk around the block and talk about our normal stuff - trees, birds, planes, trucks, and dogs. I've noticed that as her vocabulary is growing, mine is shrinking substantially. When it's finally an acceptable time to show my face I bring Little Miss inside and downstairs. She's wearing a bright green shirt that reads "soccer Star." Of course she is. I'm sizing up the competition of 16, 17 and 18 month old's when all of a sudden I smell Little Miss' brand of poo. I think to myself - "*Really*, right NOW!?" but then quickly thought it better to get it over with than interrupt her impending goal scoring. I bring her upstairs, change her diaper, and sit down to get a quick pee in myself. When I look up I think she is playing with the extra toilet paper rolls in the corner but at closer glance realize she is chewing a dog biscuit she found under the sink. Awesome P, good start. Let's get our head in the game here.

Back downstairs the group is ready to begin the "fundamentals" of soccer with Mimi and Pepe. I am loving life as the coach starts to put out mini cones for the kids to run around. It takes all of my strength not to circle them myself and kick every single ball into the little nets. I'd just be so GOOD at it. The kids are let loose and start to charge towards the cones, winding up before they let the balls fly all around the room. It's as if I was back on my high school field with the sweet smell of shin guard and leather soccer ball, flooding back. I officially turn into a deranged parent. "Go for it Little Miss!! Kick kick kick! No like THIS! See? Not with your HANDS, your FEET. FEEEEEEET. Kick Little Miss, Kick. Use your Toes! Where's your shoes? Your SHOOOOES!!" I can't stop myself; I'm so annoying.

After showing her 9 times how to kick the ball and watching in dismay as each times she picks up the ball and carries it into the net, she finally gives me a look like I'm nuts and starts waving goodbye to everyone in the room, shouting "BYE! TAnk U! Bye-BYE! Alllll doneeee" as she struts towards the door. My shoulders shrinking in disappointment I go over, pick her up, and drop her into the ball pit to have her own fun. Except she is done with balls. She instead walks over to the only mirror in the room and starts checking herself out, spinning in front of it. She heads over to the stereo and starts shaking her head a la' A Night At The Roxbury to the music. She finds a red-headed boy chasing soccer balls with his feet (show-off) and blows him multiple kisses. Parenting is a humbling experience, folks. Hope Solo she was not. But man did my little girl poop, flirt, dance, and eat a dog biscuit like the best of 'em.

Please don't tell my husband.

chapter twenty-six

TALES FROM THE LABOR AND DELIVERY ROOM

chapter twenty-six

Disclaimer to 1st time pregnant women:
1.) Everyone experiences labor differently. Don't go in with any expectations.
2.) There is no one right way to deliver a baby; there is only your way.

April 21st, 2011 9PM

I'm 19 hours into labor enjoying a magical thing called Mr. Epidural when Nurse Buzzkill tells me that it's almost time to start pushing. She comes over to stick her hand up my crotch and I don't feel a damn thing. I think: Sweet! If I can't feel her fat forearm go up then I *definitely* won't feel a baby come down. I'm golden. Hubby is in the ready position, holding my right knee. Nurse Buzzkill lets us know that the baby is still Sunny Side Up and I'll need to push just to flip her before I push to get her out. Trying to ignore the fact that she referred to our baby as a common breakfast dish AND the fact that I'd be pushing for no apparent progress towards getting to meet that breakfast anytime soon; I inquire where the Doctor is. I detect a small snort before she answers "Doc only shows up for the big show." Mkay. So I start to push, and push, and push and I'm thinking this isn't so bad. But then enter Buzzkill who tells me it's not working. I'm crestfallen. I thought I was doing so well. I feel defeated and way too sorry for myself for only having pushed for 15 minutes. Why didn't I get Nurse Warm & Fuzzy back for this part? I know her shift was over and all, but didn't she want to stay and help me through this? Surely she couldn't have something more important to do? And here I had thought we became best friends.

Back at the ranch Buzzkill tells me to roll over on my side because apparently pushing in that position will help turn the baby face down. I look at her like her ass went Sunny Side Up. First, there is no way I can move my 200lb body anywhere and Second that position was not a good look for me. I feel like a whale on a forklift as the two of them work to put me on my side.

Did I just see a bead of sweat on Hubby's forehead?

After 5 big pushes I get to lie back down taking the embarrassment level from 100 to 50. I guess it worked and Little Miss was now over easy.

The contractions are coming quicker than ever and I'm starting to feel them like never before. I have this little thingy in my hand that lets me turn up Mr. Epidural when I feel the pain come on. I never used it once in the 19 hours of "inactive" (Worst Term Ever) labor but now I'm pushing that thing like I'm in an epic battle of Tetris on level 29. It's not working. I ask why and Buzzkill replies: "it's probably wearing off." I'm sorry, come again? She repeats more loudly than necessary, "IT'S PROBABLY WEARING OFF." But can't we get that handsome resident fellow with the Boston College scrubs back down here to give me another dose? No dice. I'm in panic mode. The contractions start low and build high. It feels like I'm biking up a mountain and then hit a part of it so steep that I can't pedal anymore and my legs are about to give out. Except they can't give out because I don't have control over them, they are moving without me and that hill is happening no matter what. I'm entangled in a sheet of white pain so intense I think I might pass out. And then it releases, slowly, and I'm headed back downhill. I look up at my husband and want nothing more than to be standing where he is at this very moment. I ask for water and chapstick and he returns with both before I get the words out. He is so calm. I grab his hand and tell him to never let go. He strokes my head and tells me he never will. I'm climbing the hill again; I can't take it. I beg for Gatorade for the 5th time. Nurse Buzzkill snaps back "You can keep asking me sweetheart; but the answer won't change." I'm on hour two of active labor when the Doctor finally comes in. She tells me my delivery has been text book; that my body was made for it. Two things run through my head - 1. This shit show is TEXTBOOK? and 2. I'm not sure that's a compliment.

She tells me she'll be back in 30 minutes to start the delivery and I lose it. I cannot do this for another 30 minutes, I can't even do it for another five. Mr. E packed up and left me, the bastard, and now I have no line of defense. I'm helpless. I can't believe this is happening to me. Hubby puts a cold washcloth over my eyes and I love him for it. Nurse Buzzkill inquires for the 3rd time if I'd like a mirror to check my progress down there; to which I snap back, "You can keep asking me *sweetheart* but the answer won't change."

The Doctor is back and getting suited up with gloves and a mask so I'm guessing this is "show time." I'm pushing with what I think is all my might feeling sorry for myself the entire time. And then I realize that Buzzkill is starting down at me. We lock eyes and she whispers "Okay Kristin. You can either push like you've been pushing for the last couple of hours and we'll be here for another four or you can push like you mean it and I'll get you out of here in 20 minutes." I want to hug her and punch her in the face at the same time. It's exactly what I needed to hear. So I stop wallowing in my pity, bare down, and give her the positive pushing she was asking for. 18 minutes later Little Miss' head popped out. I throw my own head back on the pillow and she is on my belly. I suck in my breath. I feel a lightness I hadn't felt in 5 months. I look down and see Hubby's eyes and think it's the coolest thing in the world.

I asked him to read this and tell me if it's how he remembers it. Here's what he said:

"Yeah. But the Boston College resident wasn't that handsome."

chapter twenty-seven

HEADS.
I MEAN TALES.
HAVE YOU SEEN
MY BRAIN?

chapter twenty-seven

I spend 3 full days with my daughter during the week. That means I'm talking Toddler-ease for 12 hours a day. That's 36 hours of rolling up my sleeves, getting down on my knees, and playing... hard. In full disclosure I just had to use a calculator to figure that out.

Little Miss is non-stop. She is engaging and curious and determined and I love it. But that's not easy work. And because I enjoy seeing the look of glee on her face when she discovers something new, I kill myself to come up with activities to keep her stimulated. Sometimes they work, sometimes they don't. Like the other day when I introduced Play-Doh for the first time thinking I'm about to slay at least an hour with colorful doughy fun. But after spending 10 minutes setting everything up and plopping her down in front of it I got a lousy 4 minutes in before she dramtically announced "ALLLLLLLL DONEEEEE" and walked away. Sigh.

Thankfully the chalk project we invented went over much better.

And luckily girl can get real creative with a sheet of stickers.

At the time of me writing this, I was working two days in an office with adults. Real, live, dressed adults. Sometimes it took me a good hour just to figure out how to talk to them. Once I talked to my first live adult of the week I would often just sit there after, mouth wide open, with a little drool coming out.

Basically, I serve Mommy-Brain Mush up all day long. Here's a little recap of my week so you know what Mush tastes like:

Last Friday I walked in to get our dry cleaning...paid... and walked out without it. I got half way down the block when I saw a number I didn't recognize on my cell phone and didn't answer it. Turns out I will walk 7 blocks home before listening to the dry cleaning clerk tell me the obvious. Mush.

On Monday I went grocery shopping with Little Miss. The groceries were scanned and in bags waiting to be taken home . I had two people with big carts full of frozen groceries waiting behind me and a check-out clerk that was less than amused. Who has 2 thumbs and left their wallet at home? This Momhole. Panicking, I spend 2 minutes (a long time in this situation) rummaging through my bag and thankfully find a blank check with a 7 year old address on it. Accepted. Mush.

I was sitting in a meeting on Tuesday and naturally, the election came up. I wanted so badly to participate and be engaged. Desperately tired from being up with a sick child the night before, I pathetically offer: "SO, I was trying to think who else from Boston has ever run for President and couldn't think of anyone. Does anyone know?" I got a bunch of sympathetic, awkward stares back at me for what seemed like a long while before someone finally leaned over and whispered "Um, Kennedy, for one." Dear, God. Mush.

This morning on my way to daycare, I drove through a Dunkin Donuts drive-thru while it was raining. I rolled the window down to give my order than rolled it up for the short drive to the pay window. Little Miss had just chirped "COCKEY!" apparently recognizing my ordering voice. I was so excited and yelled back "Yes Honey That's Right, MAMA'S ordering COFFEE!" As I pulled up to the pay area, (with my window still rolled up) I turned to the right to take my credit card out of my wallet and turned back to the left to hand it to the lady but smashed it into the car window instead. Lady dies of laughter. Hand throbs. Face red. Mush.

Other random examples of how my once fairl sophisticated mind has now turned to Mommy Mush:

- I have no idea how old I am.

- I can't, for the life of me, remember what comes after "If that diamond ring don't shine." This is Little Miss's favorite nighttime song so lately I've been making up my own lyrics: "If that diamond ring don't shine, Mama's gonna buy you a porcupine. And if that porcupine isn't Hmmm, Mama's gonna buy you some Turpentine."

- People ask me how many teeth Little Miss has all of the time. I hate this question because I never have any idea and it makes me feel dumb. I often feel like asking back: Do you know how many teeth *YOU* have?

- Today I came home to my cleaning lady holding a statue we got on our wedding day from a couple who lived in Brasil. She was holding the head with one hand and the body with the other saying "sorry" in Portuguese (ironically). I started laughing out loud. The head was sliced clean off. My endearing, sweet little daughter did not take the decapitation very well. She couldn't stop staring and with a broken face whined "WHOA NO MAMA." Sans Super Glue, I tried to make the best out of it.

And now I'm sitting here staring at the statue thinking, "I hear you Lady, I hear you."

chapter twenty-eight

DUCK TALES

chapter twenty-eight

We thought it would be fun to take Miss P. to go feed the ducks in the Boston Common today. It's cold, but nothing a big pink parka and purple hat can't handle. After searching the nether regions of our refrigerator to find some stale bread we were all in the car on the way to the park listening to the "Wheels on The Bus" for the trillionth time. Mid way through a "move on back" I looked down at the bread and realized it had a blue hue to it. Upon further inspection I saw that it was covered in blue mold. (Yes, this speaks volumes for my lack of refrigeration organization.)

Me: "Is it okay to feed ducks moldy bread?"
Hubby: "I don't know, Google it."

Commence the Google search.

Me: "AH! You aren't supposed to feed ducks bread at all! It can lead to malnutrition, disease, and behavior problems." I will not be responsible for a bad duck. "It says we should feed them lettuce instead."

Hubby has a field day with this and rambles on about even the Google search engine turning "hippy dippy."

Commence the purchase of an organic head of lettuce.

Back in the car...

Hubby: "Wait. It's Winter. Don't birds fly south?"
Me: "Crap."

Commence the drive around the pond in search of a duck that decided not to join his friends. (Maybe he was fed moldy bread and branded with bad behavior.) Spotted.

Outside the car...

Hubby: "Wanna feed the ducks sweetheart!?"
Miss P: "Duck! Yessh!"
Me: "What do ducks say, P?"
Miss P: "Woof! Moooo!"
Hubby: "Close enough! Duuuucks!"

Commence the duck chant between Hubby and Miss P. for the next five blocks: "Ducks! Ducks! Ducks!" where we were greeted with the following sign:

chapter twenty-nine

DECEMBER TALES: Glitter & Guilt

chapter twenty-nine

I love to buy things but I'm not a fan of Christmas. The whole "Be A Good Boy/Girl Or Santa Won't Come" drives me nuts. What happened to being good for the sake of being intrinsically good? Hubby rolls his eyes. I also struggle with the guilt that Christmas makes me feel. As a kid I would cry in my room for hours after opening gifts on Christmas morning. I cried for the kids who didn't get gifts at all that morning, it was depressing. Hubby is cross-eyed. Also, Christmas comes with a lot of glitter and I can't stand glitter. Christmas stuff is usually cheesy and red and green aren't colors that even go together. I passed a bum on the street the other day shaking a cup and grumbling "Merry Fucking Christmas." I wanted to scream "YES! THANK YOU!"

Hubby obviously thinks I'm a heathen and refuses to let our daughter grow up hating Christmas. We were in Home Depot the other day looking for a Christmas Tree when he took a sharp turn with the cart into the ornament aisle. Practically exploding with glee he kept trying to put acetate packages of glitter balls in our cart. I kept taking them out. After hearing my anti-glitter rant for the 100th time he turns around and yells, "It's Christmas!! Glitter is SUPPOSED to be all over the house!" He scoops Miss P. out of the cart, spins her around, and points out all of the blowup dolls overhead. I avert my eyes so cheese doesn't drip in them.

I know Hubby's right. I want my daughter to love and experience the magic of Christmas. I'd just like her to do it guilt and glitter free. I will admit seeing her eyes light up at her first "TIS-MEE TEE!" made my icy disposition melt. So here I am, going balls to the wall Christmas. Literally.

Oh, why are they still in the packaging you ask? This is called a compromise people. Hubby gets to keep his balls and I stay glitter free.

Back to my original statement: I love to buy things. So here's is what's on my Christmas list to myself year. Merry Fucking Christmas to me.

BARE MINERALS by BARE ESCENTUALS

Pre-kid, my beauty routine used to take me an hour. I was meticulous. Now I'm lucky if I get deodorant under my left armpit and eyeliner under my right eye. Enter Bare Escentuals. They offer great tools to make you look like a human being in less than 60 seconds. My favorites: "Well-Rested" (Because Lord knows I'm not) and "Fab in a Flash." Thanks for understanding, Bare Escentuals.

Exfolikate by Kate Sommerville

Every time I get a facial (like, once a year) the Estethician casually asks "So, what are you using to exfoliate?" I never had an answer, until I met Kate. I use this sucker once a week, just a dab. It gives my skin a healthy glow and gets rid of the "Oh, you must not sleep well" look. You can actually feel it working and it smells like pumpkin. I kinda wish it was edible.

CRISTALLISTE BY KERASTASE / MY HAIRDRESSER

I have long hair that I will never cut. I made that bet with my hair dresser when I became pregnant. She thought for sure I would be like everyone else and come in 8 months pregnant begging her to chop my hair off. But here I am, Little Miss turning the corner on 2 years old and my hair is still long.

Cristalliste is the only product that actually works for my long hair. It gives me that Kardashian Redheaded Stepchild look I'm striving for.

I get my layers/ends cut once every 6 months. I try to plan it before a big night out which is perfect because I usually have one of those every 6 months too. Alex Craig works at Bradley & Diegel on Newbury

Street which made Best of Boston 2012. She is the only stylist I've had that doesn't try to convince me to do something I don't really want. Hubby never noticed a haircut until I started going to her.

MY MASSEUSE

I know that sounds obnoxious but let me explain. For 18 months after delivery my body was in pain. Little Miss is 20 months old and my body is just now feeling back to normal. When I was pregnant I treated myself to a twice a month massage. I figured I wasn't spending money on wine so why not. I found Frances Masterson at Isis Parenting (now at Bodywaves in Boston's North End) and dear God did that woman know her way around a pregnant body. I never felt more calm than I did on her table. And that's important because your boobs will probably fall on either side of it.

chapter thirty

TALES FROM DATE NIGHT

chapter thirty

We were driving in the car the other day listening to Toddler Favorites when "I'm a Little Teapot" came on. Hubby said: "There's something about this song that seems really dirty." I hope you are all now singing the lyrics in your head and laughing your ass off because I did. His comment made me think we desperately needed a night out alone - sans nursery rhythms, diaper bags, kids menus and highchairs. Just us, alcohol, and semi-coherent adult conversation.

Little known fact that Hubby and I have known each other since diapers. Our parents were best friends at the University of Vermont in the late 60's. Post college, the four of them (plus a couple of stragglers) all lived together in Boston. Some may call this type of arrangement a hippie-commune but they refer to it as "budget living." (Tomato/Tomahhhto).

My now Father-In-Law was my Dad's Best Man. Here is a picture from that wedding. Don't they look like a Simon and Garfunkel cover band?

After we were born my parents moved to Up-state New York but we still saw saw each other every year for family vacations. One time we met up to go skiing when I was 12 and Future-Hubby was 13. My hair was in a ponytail the whole day as I sped down the slopes with him and my sister. His mom tells me that when we met up for dinner later that night my hair was down. Future-Hubby saw this and ran back upstairs to douse himself in Cool Water cologne. Now, I don't remember what I had for breakfast this morning let alone a story from the early 90s; however, I married Rain Man and he remembers it along with this one: He was visiting us from Boston when I was 4 and he was 5. I had already learned how to ride a bike but he hadn't yet (city kids.) Apparently I was showing off gunning it up and down the hill but no one was paying attention because they were focused on him trying to learn how to pedal alone. When he finally mastered it, everyone clapped. My bossy-ass ran over and announced "Now you have to clap as loud as you did for HIM as you do for ME" as I got back up on my bike and sped down the hill. (I would deny this but it sounds way too much like me... sonofa'...)

Anyway, I guess this is a long, disjointed way of telling you that I married my best friend. We had a blast growing up together and a blast entering adulthood together. It's so easy to forget that you married your best friend when life happens. Especially when you are all-consumed (in the best way possible) with a life you created together. I implore you all to get out of the house together, sans child, before nursery rhythms start sounding naughty.

I have recently become obsessed with UrbanSitter.com. It's free to sign up and I can read ratings, have a conversation back and forth with potential sitters, and see who else in my circle of friends has used them. The best part for me is that there is always someone available to book last minute. Like when your baby is sleeping and you get the urge to go down the street for a drink with Hubby to reminisce about the good old days when you dominated him in skiing and riding bikes.

chapter thirty-one

FOOT IN MOUTH TALES

chapter thirty-one

The MIM edition of WHAT NOT TO SAY
To a new mom or pregnant woman

"A closed mouth gathers no foot."

10.   "Your baby is beautiful.   Does she look like your husband?"

9.   "I'm so surprised your baby didn't get (eye color, eye shape, hair color, hair style, freckles, moles, temperament, nailbeds, bellybutton, left ear, third toe, etc.) Everyone knows that no one knows what a baby is going to look like when they come out. You are just as surprised as everyone else. Almost 2 years later and I'm still being asked: "Why didn't Miss P get your red hair?" This will likely be my answer the next time this happens: "We planned it that way to spare her a lifetime of idiotic carrot-top/fire crotch/ stepchild jokes. Duh."

8.   "When are you having another baby?" When people ask you this right after birth you want to cry. When they ask you a year after birth you feel like you're being pressured. When they ask you two years after birth you want to punch them in the labia.

7.   "How long did you breastfeed for?" Hey Boob-Police...no one invited you.

6.   "When are you due?" And/or "Congrats on your pregnancy!" A woman MUST confirm pregnancy first before you utter these words. The only other option here is to witness a baby coming out of her vagina. Then by all means congratulate her.

5.   "Blah, Blah, Blah, Work." Never ask a new mom her plans for going back to work, if she's heard from work, who is filling in for her at work, how long she has for maternity leave from work, or anything remotely related whatsoever to the notion of work. It's too overwhelming and emotional of a topic to talk about.

4.   "You look tired." Thank you Captain Obvious.

3.   "Did you deliver naturally?" I so badly want to respond: "No I did not delivery naturally, the baby came out of my Anus." If you MUST know whether or not a woman took pain medication during her delivery it's a three step process: 1. Ask yourself why you care. 2. Ask the question without a tone (you know who you are.) 3. Never judge the response.

2.   "Did you plan the pregnancy?" You would not believe how common this question is from normal, smart people. Here's a couple of ways you could answer it: "Yes, we were banging like jackrabbits planning this kid, thanks for asking!" Or, "No we didn't... BUMMER, huh?"

1.   "Are you sure you're not carrying twins? Here's

what to do if someone asks you this: Take the foot of that someone, place directly in that someone's mouth; preferably with shoe on.

chapter thirty-two

TALES FROM THE MASSAGE TABLE

chapter thirty-two

Despite what this title might suggest I did not accidentally shit on the massage table. Sometimes I ask Hubby to rub my shoulders and he does it so poorly that I end up begging him to stop. He acts surprised like he thought he was doing a good job but I know it's his master plan to never have to give a back rub longer than 60 seconds. He sent me to get a massage yesterday because I've been complaining about major neck and shoulder pain. Apparently lifting 30lbs up and down three flights of stairs all day isn't that great for your upper body. I would have really appreciated a stair-lift but hey, you take what you can get, right?

I had a total of 60 minutes before Miss P. would be up from her nap looking for me so I cheated on my go-to, affordable Bodywaves Therapeutic Massage in the North End of Boston and went down the street to a no-name spa instead. In the words of Vivian Ward: "Big Mistake. Huge."

Right when I walked into the room the woman asked me a question that I don't even remember. But I guess my answer had the word "masseuse" in it because she interrupted me to tell me that the correct term is "massage THERAPIST." Whatever lady, I didn't make you call me a domestic engineer did I? Give me a break. I laid down on the bed and tried to "let go" but the sheets were so cold it hurt my boobs. So I tried to focus on the music but quickly realized it was old Christmas songs without lyrics. The worst. Plus It's February for Christ's sake. (I think that pun was intended.) She starts the massage and her hands are so dry they scratch my skin. I didn't ask for an exfoliation. And then she starts talking...and talking...and talking. I was giving her one word mumbled responses to try and make an obvious point to no avail. What I wanted to remind her is that she wasn't an ACTUAL therapist and to stop asking me about my childhood. It was a 60 minute massage. 40 of those excruciating minutes were spent on one knot in the center of my back. Sure, that knot is gone but 4 more cropped up in protest. I should have stayed home, tied a sack of potatoes around my torso and asked Hubby to rub my shoulders while I marched up and down the stairs. It would have made for a much nicer experience.

chapter thirty-three

SELFLESS TALES: *It's Not About You Anymore*

chapter thirty-three

    I have a friend that is nervous about getting pregnant because she still has her own issues to work through. I told her that's the perfect time to get pregnant because once the baby comes she won't even have time to think about them. Like most people, before having a baby I was completely self-consumed. It was all about me. But not anymore. I was shopping with my mother recently, helping her look for a Mother Of The Bride's dress for daughter number three. I watched as the sales woman in Neiman Marcus doted on her for hours. And the whole time I thought to myself, my God does she deserve this. Now that her kids are grown up she finally has "me-time" after giving up so much of herself to raise daughters. It made me think of the things that have changed in my life just after a short two years...

- I used to consider it a successful day when I sailed through a presentation, answered all 75 emails, and got at least 60 minutes in at the gym. But these days I measure success in different ways. If I look down at my hands before bed and see marker residue and a left-over Dora sticker I consider it a win. (Even if the reason my hands are dirty is because I didn't get to shower that day.)

- I used to love reading gossip magazines while taking a long steamy bubble bath. Now I read "The Happiest Toddler On The Block" on the rare occasion I get to take a crap alone.

- I used to manage my meals. I planned my breakfast every night before work. I made sure to pack healthy snacks like cut-up apples and nuts in plastic bags for the car ride. I always knew where my lunch was coming from and took pride in cooking lavish meals for Hubby and I at night. I hate to sit and it gave me something to do when I got home, plus it was a nice excuse to drink wine. But now this attention to food management has entirely shifted to the needs of Little Miss. I practically kill myself to make sure she's getting the right roods during the day. And some days that feels like a full time job. Meanwhile this has wrecked havoc on my diet. Today for example I had the 3 blueberries that fell out of her bib, a half an apple because she wanted to share it with me, 5 bites of left-over whole wheat organic Mac & Cheese (which she insisted on feeding to me) and an uneaten half of a veggie burger post night-time routine.

- I used to spend money on me, but now it all goes to Miss P. New clothes, toys, and shoes every week. I just can't stop myself. Diapers.com doesn't help my situation. They make it way too easy to shop from my couch along with free shipping. There's a new box on our doorstep practically daily. I've considered inviting the UPS guy in for coffee. At the mall with mom, I passed right by Banana Republic and spent a half an hour at the Baby Gap instead.

- I used to be really good about getting enough sleep. I would aim for 7 hours, every night. But now I can never remember how many hours I got because I'm usually up wondering if Miss P. is getting her adequate shut-eye. The focus has completely shifted. I've been this way since she was born. I've been called the Nap Nazi and I deserve it.

Hubby loves to quote movies and TV shows. When we first started dating I thought he was witty. But than as he eventually made me suffer through some of his favorites, I began to realize that his clever remarks were all stolen lines. I was the first one to tell him that I loved him. He answered me with: "Wow. That's a BIG Matzo ball to put out there..." (hand cupping the air). Any diehards out there will know that is a quote taken directly from Seinfeld; a fact that I did not know at the time. I just thought he was a weirdo and (thankfully) too drunk to remember the conversation the next day.

Anyway, one of his favorite lines is from The Girl Next Door, when the nice kid is explaining moral fiber after scoring the porn star (if you haven't seen the movie don't ask). The "Juice was Worth the Squeeze" he says. And that's how I feel here. This post is not a complaint but an observation. When I put in my all, my 100%; I get 200 back from Miss P. The juice is absolutely worth the squeeze. I look forward to one day shopping with her, when she's a new mom herself. I'll be enjoying the luxury of time and smiling just a little when I see her walk past the J.Crew into a Baby Gap.

chapter thirty-four

TALES FROM MY BELLY

chapter thirty-four

As Miss P. rounds the corner of two years old, here are some of the thoughts that are going through my mind...

    I always knew that becoming a mother would change me. But not like this. People say time goes by quickly and on some level it has; but to me her birth seems like forever ago. We've done so much living in 2 short years. I get a such a deep sense of nostalgia thinking her first birthday.
    I will never ever tire of watching her experience things for the first time. It's fascinating, and fun, and all-consuming in the best way. The layers of love I keep finding for her within myself are endless. How lucky I am to have that special feeling be mine forever.

The little things I love about you, Missy Moo, now that you are two:

The way you smile with your whole face

How proud and brave you are when you go to school

The creative ways you play

Your uninhibited displays of happiness

The way you love your daddy

And For All Our Misadventures Together...

We can't wait to introduce you to your new sister or brother this Fall...

Happy 2nd Birthday, my little muse,
Miss Paigely Baker Quinn

About the (fab) Author

After graduating from Boston University in 2001, Kristin Quinn moved to New York to work for *Martha Stewart* where she helped plan and implement an exclusive product line into Kmart stores for three years. After, she moved to Chicago and sold sophisticated high-functioning coffee mugs into *Starbucks Corporate*. Two years later Kristin moved back to Boston and worked with *Dorel Industries* - purveyors of the following powerhouse baby brands: *Quinny*, *Maxi-Cosi*, *Cosco*, and *Safety 1st*. There she served as both a Senior Product Manager and Senior Channel Manager developing products and introducing brands to retailers like *Babies R Us*, *Walmart*, *Target*, *Sears*, and *Specialty Retailers*. In 2012 she left to fulfill her dream of running a yoga studio in Boston and is now the owner of *Charlestown Yoga*. She is a featured writer for the website *Mommy Poppins Boston* and a contributing writer to *Beantown Mom* magazine. She is the author of Misadventures in Mommyhood, a popular humor blog with both a national and international audience helping to bring "the truth & nothing but the truth" to everyday moms. Her work has been featured in *Boston Magazine*. She lives in Boston with her husband, Sam and their daughter, Paigely. She is due in October 2013 with their second child.

Made in the USA
Charleston, SC
15 August 2013